Francisco Vásquez de Coronado

A Proud Heritage The Hispanic Library

Francisco Vásquez de Coronado

The Search for Cities of Gold

Carrie Nichols Cantor

Published in the United States of America by The Child's World®
PO Box 326 • Chanhassen, MN 55317-0326 • 800-599-READ • www.childsworld.com

Acknowledgments
  The Creative Spark: Mary Francis-DeMarois, Project Director; Carrie Nichols Cantor, Series
  Editor; Robert Court, Design and Art Direction
  Carmen Blanco, Curriculum Adviser
  The Child's World®: Mary Berendes, Publishing Director

Photos
  Alderman Library, University of Virginia: 10; Bettmann/CORBIS: 13; Carrie Nichols Cantor: 7,
  31; CORBIS: 9; Denver Public Library: 16, 18, 19, 21, 22, 23, 29; Philip Greenspun: 15; Dave
  Bly/NPS Photo: cover; Layne Kennedy/CORBIS: 26; Geoffrey Clements/ CORBIS: 25; David
  Muench/CORBIS: 33

Library of Congress Cataloging-in-Publication Data
  Cantor, Carrie Nichols.
  Francisco Vásquez de Coronado : the search for cities of gold / by Carrie Nichols Cantor.
  p. cm. — (A proud heritage : the Hispanic library)
  Summary: Traces the life and accomplishments of Spanish explorer and conquistador,
  Francisco Vásquez de Coronado, who led a major expedition from Mexico through what
  is now the southwestern United States.
  Includes bibliographical references and index.
  Contents: Who was Coronado?—The road to the Seven Cities—Indian friends and
  enemies—Things fall apart.
  ISBN 1-56766-210-2 (lib. bdg. : alk. paper)
  1. Coronado, Francisco Vásquez de, 1510–1554—Juvenile literature. 2. Explorers—Spain—
  Biography—Juvenile literature. 3. Explorers—America—Biography—Juvenile literature.
  4. Southwest, New—Discovery and exploration—Spanish—Juvenile literature. 5. America—
  Discovery and exploration—Spanish—Juvenile literature. [1. Coronado, Francisco Vásquez
  de,1510–1554. 2. Explorers. 3. America—Discovery and exploration—Spanish. 4. Southwest,
  New—Discovery and exploration.] I. Title. II. Proud heritage (Child's World (Firm))
  E125.V3C36 2003
  979'.01'092—dc21
  [B]   2002152665

Who Was Coronado?

Francisco Vásquez de Coronado had an adventure that was unique in history. He was born in Spain and then went to live in Mexico at a time when Europeans did not know much at all about the huge landmass that lay to the north. Coronado led a major **expedition** into this unknown territory. He had the chance to explore a completely new land. And it wasn't just any old land. It was the heartland of what would become, more than 200 years later, the United States.

Coronado was the first European to see the vast herds of buffalo that once roamed the central plains. His men were the first Europeans to view the Grand Canyon and the Painted Desert and the first to set foot in California. His group **traversed** more miles of new land than any other party of explorers. Most people look back on him with admiration and awe.

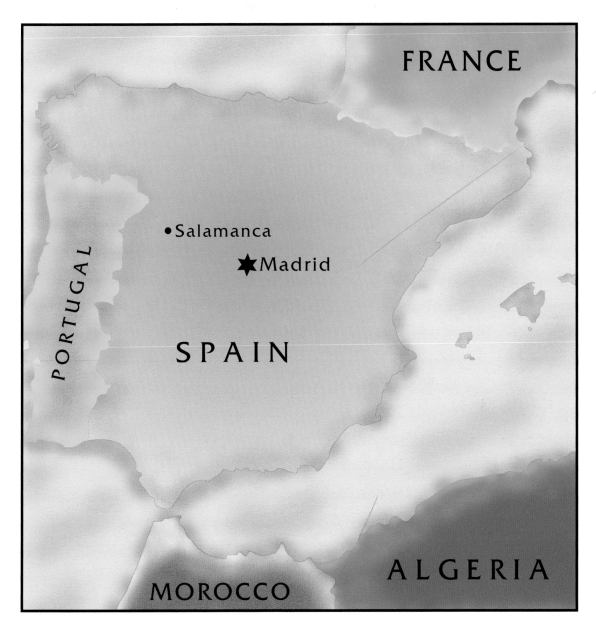

Francisco Vásquez de Coronado was born in Salamanca, Spain, in 1510.

Yet Coronado probably considered himself a failure. He did not find what he was looking for—the Seven Cities of Cíbola (SEE-bow-luh). He lost all of his money on this one expedition. He was even arrested and put on trial for mistreating Native Americans. He was removed from his position as governor of New Galicia. And he died while still a young man. Yet 400 years later there is a national park in his honor in the United States.

The Luck of the Spanish

Francisco Vásquez de Coronado was born in Salamanca, Spain, in 1510, only 18 years after Spain discovered and claimed the Americas. Christopher Columbus had stumbled on it while looking for Asia. He sailed west from Spain, expecting to find a new route to India. Because he thought he had succeeded, he called the people he met "Indians." Years later, the Spanish realized that Columbus had instead discovered a continent entirely unknown to Europeans. No one knew how vast a territory it would turn out to be.

Spanish **conquistadors** took these lands by force from the people who lived there. They found and stole great quantities of gold, silver, and other valuables, which they brought home to Spain. Spain became the wealthiest country in the world.

Coronado was part of a rich, well-known Spanish family. But because he was his father's second son, his family's land would go to his older brother. Francisco knew he would have to earn his own fortune. Luckily for him, a friend of his family's, Antonio de Mendoza, was appointed by the king of Spain to be the **viceroy** of New Spain—the area that is now the country of Mexico. He would rule New Spain for the king. Mendoza invited Coronado to come with him. He gave him the job of governor of the province of New Galicia. While living in

This drawing shows the meeting between the Spanish explorer Hernán Cortés and the Aztec leader Montezuma in Tenochtitlan (later renamed Mexico City) in 1519. The Spanish conquered the Aztecs and made the city their capital in the Americas.

In the center of this 16th-century map is a large island labeled "Cuba." The large landmass above it is supposed to be what is now the United States and Canada. But it doesn't look anything like the real thing. No one in Coronado's time knew how large the North American continent was.

Mexico, Coronado married a beautiful and rich young lady named Beatriz de Estrada.

At only 28 years old, Coronado was now both wealthy and powerful. He could have decided to live a quiet, happy, safe life, raising children and enjoying his good fortune. But instead he chose adventure.

Chapter Two

The Road to the Seven Cities

In 1536, Coronado heard a true story that he couldn't stop thinking about. Four skinny, exhausted men wearing animal skins had been found on the west coast of Mexico. Three were Spaniards, and one was an African named Esteban. They said they had been lost in the wilderness north of Mexico for eight long years. They had been part of a 400-man expedition that started out in Florida in 1528. The leader of the expedition, Álvar Núñez Cabeza de Vaca, was one of the survivors. The four men had been shipwrecked on the coast of Texas. They had lived among a number of different Native American tribes while walking toward the west, hoping to find home. Their survival seemed miraculous.

One part of their story especially interested Coronado and Mendoza. The survivors said they had heard from the Native Americans about rich cities to the north filled with gold. They were called the Seven Cities of Cíbola. Coronado, Mendoza, and other Spaniards hearing this story imagined another large country, like Mexico, with great cities and enormous wealth that the Spaniards could conquer.

Did these golden cities really exist? Mendoza's first step was to send a small **scouting party** north to try to get more information quickly. He sent Esteban, the African who had been one of the four survivors. To accompany Esteban were three priests, one of whom was named Fray Marcos de Niza, as well as about 60 other men.

Five months later, Fray Marcos returned but Esteban did not. He had been killed by Native Americans. Fray Marcos had fled home in fear. But he said he had been to a place called Cíbola. He said that from a distance he saw a huge city with ten-story buildings and doors decorated with turquoise. Native Americans had told him that there was gold in the Seven Cities of Cíbola.

The Adventure Begins

Mendoza and Coronado were very excited. They each put up huge amounts of their own money and started planning an expedition to Cíbola. Mendoza chose Coronado to lead it.

Coronado set off from Compostela, Mexico, with about 1,000 men.

On February 22, 1540, more than 300 soldiers and 700 Native Americans gathered in the city of Compostela, Mexico, to start the journey of a lifetime. History has provided us with a remarkable thing: a written list of the names of Coronado's men and what they brought with them. According to this list, Coronado brought a golden suit of armor and a helmet with a feather as well as 23 horses and several suits of horse armor. Most of the soldiers rode on horseback but some walked. Many sheep and pigs were brought along to serve as sources of food.

Fray Marcos and a few other priests had already begun the journey. Viceroy Mendoza was a new sort of Spanish ruler in the Americas. He intended for this expedition to be guided by Christian values of peace and humanity. On other occasions, Spaniards had been violent toward Native Americans. Mendoza ordered Coronado to treat all Native Americans "as if they were Spaniards." Yet, at the same time, he thought of the Native Americans as primitive people who needed to be saved.

After a parade, a religious ceremony, and a speech by Viceroy Mendoza, the men set off. Hopes were high that vast riches lay ahead. Coronado knew that if his expedition was successful, he would be rich, famous, and highly respected.

Much of the terrain the group passed through was rocky, steep, and barren. By April the group had gone only 300 miles (480 kilometers) and was running low on food. Coronado decided to move ahead more quickly with 100 of his best men. The rest were to catch up later.

The First Disappointments

When they crossed into what is now the state of Arizona, Coronado and his 100 men soon came to a harsh and barren area the Spaniards called the *despoblado,* a wilderness with little food or water. They trudged on, believing they would soon reach a town called Chichilticali that Fray Marcos had said was home to several thousand people. Fray Marcos turned out to be wrong about many things. The "town" was just a single mud hut. It was a devastating disappointment for the hungry, thirsty men.

Finally they reached Hawikuh, the first of the Seven Cities of Cíbola. They expected to see a rich, beautiful city with many big buildings and thousands of wealthy Native Americans wearing fancy jewelry. What they saw

The Coronado expedition traveled through harsh terrain, including deserts.

The Native Americans of Cíbola built pueblos—towns of rectangular adobe houses all clustered together.

was a cluster of rectangular houses made of mud and surrounded by an **adobe** wall. The houses were bunched together, some on top of the others. They were plain, with cutout squares for windows. They were the dingy color of dust. No gold or any other precious metals were seen. Hawikuh, home to about 800 people, was just a humble little village.

Chapter Three

Native American Friends and Enemies

The people who lived in Hawikuh were Zuni Native Americans. On seeing the strangers, they poured corn-meal on the ground in the shape of a line that the Spaniards were not supposed to cross. The Spaniards believed it was their right to claim all the new lands they reached for the king of Spain. Coronado read the Native Americans something called the *requerimiento*, which Spanish conquerors were required to read when they came upon any native peoples. It informed the Native Americans that they were now **subjects** of the king of Spain and were expected to convert to Christianity.

The Zuni needed more than a requerimiento to convince them. They must have been awed by the large, unfamiliar beasts many of the intruders sat on and by their metal armor and guns. Even so, they shot arrows at them.

The Battle of Hawikuh, the first of many battles between Europeans and Native Americans, began. Such a turn of events was not what the Spaniards wanted. They had hoped to make peace right away. But they fought back, not only to **subdue** the Zuni but also because they needed the food and water within the village walls.

The Zuni fought by throwing large rocks and shooting arrows out of bows. They aimed at Coronado in particular because he was clearly the group's leader. He had the fanciest suit of armor, and he had read them the requerimiento. Coronado was knocked to the ground twice and fell unconscious. He was saved from death by two of his top men, Garcia López de Cardenas and Hernando de Alvarado, who pulled him out of harm's way.

The Zuni kept up the fight for about an hour until they ran out of rocks and arrows. Then they fled into the hills. No Spaniards died, though a few

Above is a portrait of a Taos Pueblo man taken in the 1890s. He holds a bow and arrows.

These Zuni women, photographed in New Mexico around 1900, are dressed in elaborate costumes. The women in the background carry large ceramic jars of water balanced on their heads.

Zuni did. Coronado and his men finally got to eat, drink, and think about what to do next. When the rest of his forces finally arrived in Hawikuh, Coronado sent out small groups of soldiers to capture the nearby Zuni villages. The Seven Cities of Cíbola were seven poor towns, all as disappointing to the Spaniards as Hawikuh.

Eventually the Zuni made peace with the Spaniards. Coronado and his men got to know some of the Zuni people and became familiar with their way of life. There were many things they admired about them, such as the way they farmed and the things they made.

Exploring in Different Directions

Coronado heard from some Zuni that there were other towns to the northwest where he would find gold and other precious items. Coronado was still recovering from his battle wounds and could not travel. So that summer he sent out several small groups in different directions to see what might be worth exploring.

One group of 20 men headed west for 75 miles (120 kilometers) to the region of Tuzan. Hopi Native Americans lived there. Their villages were only a little larger than the ones in Cíbola. While there the Spaniards were told of a great river even farther to the west. The Spaniards returned to Hawikuh and told Coronado about it.

Coronado sent out another group, led by Cardenas, to find the river. They found it at the bottom of a spectacularly deep gorge, a trench that had been carved out of solid rock over the centuries by the river. Today this gorge is one of the biggest tourist sites in the world—the Grand Canyon. These men were the first Europeans to see this amazing natural wonder.

Another group of 25 men went west in search of the Pacific Ocean to meet a supply boat from Mexico.

The Native Americans were amazed by the beasts the Spanish rode. Eventually these strange animals would change their lives tremendously. Native Americans didn't start using horses right after Coronado arrived. But 140 years later, the Pueblo Native Americans rose up and drove the Spanish out of their land. The Spaniards left so quickly that they had to leave many of their horses.

The Pueblo began using these horses to hunt buffalo. Then they started to raise them and sell them to other Native Americans. Before they had horses, Native Americans had to carry their things or put them on a sled pulled by dogs. Horses were of such great use that Native Americans called them "sacred dogs." The Plains Native Americans became expert riders and began to use horses to make war against other tribes. Those tribes that became the most expert were able to push other tribes off their lands.

The arrival of the Spanish changed the lives of Native Americans in many ways. The use of horses was just one way. Horses made Native Americans' lives easier. Horses also changed the balance of power among the various tribes.

They crossed the Colorado River and ended up in California. They were the first Europeans to set foot in California.

Meanwhile, Native Americans had been spreading the news about the strangely dressed foreigners and their strong, fast beasts with humanlike hair along their necks. Several Native Americans from the east traveled 300 miles (480 kilometers) to meet Coronado and offer their friendship.

One of the Native Americans had a long mustache. The Spaniards nicknamed him Bigotes (the Spanish word

These Hopi men, photographed in Arizona around 1900, are performing a ceremony involving wooden wind instruments similar to flutes.

Coronado and his men met different tribes on their journey. These tribes had many things in common, particularly the way they built their houses and set up their towns. The Spanish called them Pueblo Native Americans. *Pueblo* is the Spanish word for "town." It is also the word for a big building with many rooms. Often many Native American families lived in one pueblo, which might be four or five stories tall.

The various Pueblo tribes spoke different languages and had different customs. Coronado and his men met Hopi, Taos, Jimez, Zuni, and Tigua. All of these tribes still exist today.

Pueblo Native Americans were farmers and hunters. All land was owned by the tribe, not by individual families. Each family was given the right to farm a section of land. They raised mainly maize, a kind of corn. They did not eat it off the cob, as we do today, but ground it up into flour for flat bread. They also grew beans and squash. The men hunted and the women and children collected berries and nuts.

The Pueblos grew cotton and made cloth. They created clay pots painted with lovely designs. And they grew gourds that they dried, hollowed out, and used as containers.

for "whiskers"). These visitors told Coronado about a great river in the east and huge herds of some sort of "cattle" that grazed in the plains near their home. Bigotes agreed to guide a group east to explore.

Hospitality from the Tigua

In late August, Coronado sent 20 men, led by Hernando de Alvarado, to the area they called Tiguex (TIH-go), in northeastern New Mexico (near present-day Santa Fe). Along the way they found the river they later named the Rio Grande (Great River). Along the river were 12 towns inhabited by the Tigua people. Bigotes knew exactly how to approach the different Native American communities and make peace so that the Europeans could move around without any trouble. Without his help the Spaniards might have had to fight these Native Americans.

Captain Alvarado, the leader of the Spanish group, sent messengers with a map back to Coronado. He urged him to come spend the winter along the Rio Grande among the many peaceful Native Americans, where food was plentiful.

Now Captain Alvarado was eager to see the "cattle" that roamed the plains. Bigotes wanted to remain in his hometown of Cicúye (now Pecos). But he sent two Native Americans who had been captured from another tribe to guide Alvarado in the east. The Spaniards thought one of these two men looked like he came from the Eurasian country of Turkey, so they nicknamed him "the Turk." As it turned out, it would have been better if they had never met him.

The Turk did take Alvarado to see the buffalo. Some 60 million buffalo lived in the middle of North America

Native Americans depended on buffalo for food and materials they used to make things. In Coronado's time, before the natives got horses from the Spanish, they hunted buffalo on foot. This picture was painted hundreds of years after Coronado's journey.

More than three centuries after Alvarado saw his first buffalo, Americans were fighting Native Americans all over the western and central United States for control of the land. Americans knew that Native Americans depended on the buffalo. They ate its meat and used its hide, hair, and horn to make things.

Many historians believe that the U.S. government deliberately encouraged hunters to kill off the buffalo as a way of destroying the Native Americans. Hunters in fact killed more than 3 million animals from 1872 to 1874. The famous frontiersman Buffalo Bill shot more than 4,000 of them in a year and a half. By 1899 there were only about 500 buffalo left.

Eventually conservationists became concerned. They revived the buffalo herds by setting up protected areas for them in several states. Today there are more than 10,000 buffalo living in U.S. parks.

at that time. Alvarado was stunned by the vast herds of these strange horned, humpbacked grass-eating animals. They were big and strong and killed several of his horses.

Another Story of Gold

But Alvarado was even more interested in the rich land called Quivira (KEE-vih-ruh) that the Turk kept talking about. The Turk said he came from a land farther east that was full of gold. Alvarado wasn't sure whether to believe him. He wondered why the Turk didn't have any gold jewelry himself. But the Turk claimed he owned a gold bracelet that Bigotes had taken away from him.

Alvarado rushed back to Bigotes's hometown to get him to show the bracelet and tell him about Quivira and its riches. He felt Bigotes had been keeping important information from them. Bigotes insisted that there was no bracelet and that the Turk was lying.

For some reason, Alvarado chose to believe the Turk. He put Bigotes, the great peacemaker, in chains and accused him of betrayal. He took him from his home and forced him to come with him to Tiguex to face Coronado. It was the beginning of big trouble for the expedition.

Chapter Four

Things Fall Apart

Coronado arrived in Tiguex with his army just before the first snows of winter. He and his men did not approach the Native Americans with the same sort of friendliness that Alvarado and Bigotes had shown. The first thing they did was take over an entire village, forcing its people to leave. They ate their food and wore their clothing. As more Spaniards arrived, they took things right off the backs of any Native Americans they met.

The Native Americans became angry. A group of 200 of them stole some horses. The Spaniards captured the raiders. They decided to burn all 200 of them together in a big bonfire as punishment. The Native Americans who watched this happen were horrified. It was a terrible event that would not have been approved by Viceroy Mendoza.

More Spaniards arrived, taking over other villages and burning what they didn't need. The remaining Native Americans fled to their strongest village, Moho, for safety. The Spaniards went after them.

The Spaniards decided to **lay siege** to the village. They knew if they didn't allow any food or water into the village, the Native Americans would eventually have to come out. The siege lasted the entire winter. In mid-March the Spaniards allowed the women and children trapped in Moho to leave safely. A few days later, the men tried to sneak out. The Spaniards caught and killed them all.

This photograph of Hopi Native Americans hiking up a hill in Arizona around 1900 gives an idea of the sort of terrain the Coronado expedition walked through.

Meanwhile, Alvarado arrived with Bigotes in chains. When Coronado heard the Turk's gold bracelet story, he sided with Alvarado and agreed that Bigotes was a liar. Seeing the peacemaker Bigotes as a captive only angered the Tigua people more. By now Coronado had made bitter enemies out of these once-friendly Native Americans. Perhaps if Coronado and his men had remained friendly with Bigotes, he would have helped them make peace with the Native Americans. Later Coronado would pay for these mistakes.

The Long Trek to Quivira

When spring came, Coronado was eager to move on to Quivira in search of the riches the Turk had continued to talk about all winter long. The Turk led them southeast, into Texas. But in fact Quivira was to the north, in the area we now call Kansas. After traveling 600 miles (970 kilometers) during five weeks, the Spaniards finally realized that the Turk was leading them nowhere. Finally the Turk admitted he was hoping the Spaniards and their horses would grow exhausted from wandering around. Then his own people would have the upper hand. Now it was the Turk who was put in chains.

Coronado turned to the north and continued on with 40 men in late May. He had to see Quivira for himself. A

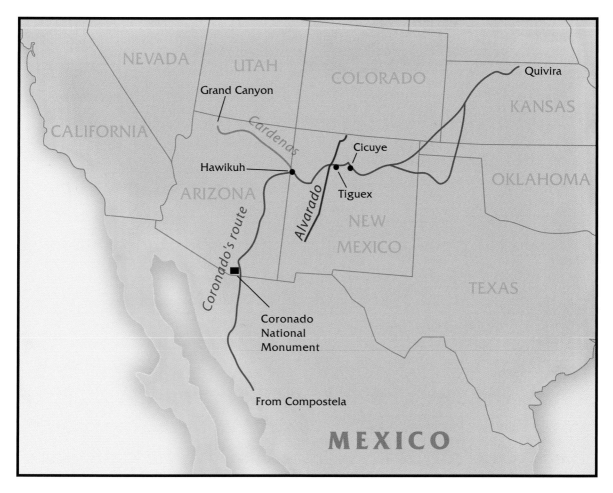

Coronado's expedition explored more miles of territory than any other. They went from Mexico through the states of Arizona, New Mexico, Texas, Oklahoma, and Kansas.

different Native American guide, named Sopete, warned them that Quivira was just a village of grass huts. When the Spaniards finally arrived there a month later, they saw that it was true. The people of Quivira didn't even know what gold was.

The disappointed Spaniards did note that Quivira was an ideal place for farming. The land was flat and the soil rich. Some of Coronado's men wanted to remain and become rich farmers. Today, the area, now known as the Wheat Belt, produces tons of grain for people all over the world.

The men remained for only a month. Coronado wanted all of his soldiers to return to Tiguex for the upcoming winter. Many of the men hoped to continue exploring the following spring.

A Tragic Accident

Back in Tiguex, there wasn't much to do while waiting for the winter to pass. To kill time the men raced each other on horseback. One day in December Coronado started racing with one of his officers. His servant had just put a new strap on his saddle to hold it in place. The strap broke during the race, and the saddle fell off, taking Coronado with it. As he fell to the ground, he was kicked hard in the head by one of the galloping horses. He suffered a serious **concussion** and nearly died. Coronado lived, but he was never quite the same again. His recovery was slow and incomplete. He was tortured with terrible pain.

When spring came, Coronado wanted to go home, even though many of his men did not. In early April 1542, the long march back to Mexico began. Coronado had to ride on a stretcher carried by two horses.

Painful Journey Home

Coronado returned home a broken man who had failed in his mission. The money he and Viceroy Mendoza had spent on the expedition had been wasted. Only 100 of Coronado's 1,000 men returned with him. Lots of soldiers had deserted, fearing the viceroy would be angry about the way they had treated the Native Americans.

They were right. Coronado was blamed for the war with the Tigua people and for the deaths of many Native

The Coronado National Memorial, a park in southern Arizona that honors the explorer, is a beautiful, unspoiled wilderness.

Americans. A couple of years later he was put on trial for those crimes and found guilty. He was removed from his post as governor of New Galicia. Coronado lost his health, his fortune, and his reputation. He died 12 years after his return to Mexico, when he was only 44 years old.

Coronado: Success or Failure?

Coronado died thinking that he was a failure. But today we recognize his achievements. He failed to find riches, but history remembers him as a daring explorer. He explored a vast section of a new continent that no European knew anything about. He trudged through harsh wilderness, desert, lava fields, and all kinds of spectacular terrain. He discovered the strange, unfamiliar humped beasts called buffalo. He met new tribes of Native Americans who had never seen white men before. He laid the foundation for the Spanish king's conquest of the American Southwest, which remained under Spanish—and then Mexican rule—until 1848.

Coronado is today honored with the Coronado National Memorial, a 5,000-acre (2,030-hectare) state park in southern Arizona at the Mexican border. It was created near the spot where the expedition crossed over from Mexico into the United States. The park is all grass and woodlands. Most of it still looks just as it did the day an

Many of the Spaniards who went to the Americas considered Native Americans less than human. As a result Native Americans were often treated with cruelty.

A Spanish priest named Bartolomé de Las Casas came to the Americas in 1510 (the year Coronado was born). He was upset by the way Native Americans were treated. He brought the problem to the king of Spain and spent the rest of his life trying to change things. He made many enemies among the Spaniards in the Americas.

Not until 1542 did the king create new laws protecting Native Americans. This was the same year Coronado returned from his expedition. These laws affected how Spanish authorities judged Coronado's crimes against Native Americans.

enormous **procession** of Spanish soldiers, Native Americans, religious men, horses, pigs, and sheep passed through to bring two completely different worlds into contact. The site of the crossing may not have changed much, but the world has never been the same since.

PORTUGAL

• Salamanca

★ Madrid

SPAIN

1492: Columbus discovers the Americas.

1510: Francisco Vásquez de Coronado is born in Salamanca, Spain.

1519–1521: Hernán Cortés conquers Mexico for Spain.

1535: Coronado goes to Mexico with Viceroy Antonio de Mendoza.

1536: Cabeza de Vaca, Esteban, and two other survivors of the Pánfilo Narváez expedition are found in western Mexico.

1538: Coronado is appointed governor of New Galicia.

1539: Esteban and Fray Marcos lead a small group north to find out what they can about the Seven Cities of Cíbola. Esteban is killed. Fray Marcos returns and claims to have seen one of the cities.

1540: In February, Coronado's expedition sets off from Compostela, Mexico, to find the Seven Cities of Cíbola.

In July, Coronado and 100 men each Hawikuh and win the battle with the Zuni Native Americans.

In August, Cardenas discovers the Grand Canyon. Alvarado and Bigotes reach the Tiguex region along the Rio Grande.

In December, Coronado and the rest of the army reach Tiguex to spend the winter there. Alvarado brings Bigotes back in chains. The siege of Moho begins.

1541: In March, the Native Americans trapped inside Moho are caught sneaking out and are killed.

In the spring, the Turk leads Coronado through northern Texas in search of Quivira.

In the summer, Coronado reaches Quivira, in present-day Kansas.

In the fall, Coronado goes back to Tiguex to spend the winter.

In December, Coronado is kicked in the head by a horse.

1542: In the spring, Coronado heads home to Mexico.

Coronado and Cardenas are tried in Mexico City for crimes at Tiguex. Coronado is found not guilty. Cardenas is found guilty and sentenced to jail.

1544: Coronado is tried again and found guilty. He loses his post as governor of New Galicia.

1554: On September 22, Coronado dies in Mexico City.

1952: The Coronado National Memorial, a park commemorating the expedition, is established near Bisbee, Arizona, near the place where Coronado and his men crossed from Mexico into what is now the United States.

adobe (uh-DOH-bee) Adobe is mud dried in the sun and cut into bricks. Many Native Americans built their homes of adobe.

concussion (kun-KUH-shun) A concussion is a head injury that results in bleeding in the brain. Coronado nearly died from a serious concussion.

conquistadors (kon-KEE-stuh-dorz) The Spanish soldiers who came to the Americas and took over the land for the king of Spain were known as conquistadors. Hernán Cortés and Francisco Pizarro were famous conquistadors.

expedition (ex-peh-DIH-shun) An expedition is a major journey undertaken by explorers. Coronado led a large expedition in the Americas.

lay siege (LAY SEEJ) To lay siege to a town is to trap the people inside and keep supplies from getting in. Eventually the people under siege have to come out or die from lack of food and water.

procession (pro-SEH-shun) A procession is a parade of people walking together in an organized way. Soldiers often walk in procession.

scouting party (SKOW-ting PAR-tee) A scouting party is a small group that runs ahead of a larger group to get information. Armies use scouting parties to sneak into areas where a large group cannot go.

subdue (sub-DOO) To subdue people is to get them under control. To subdue the Native Americans in Hawikuh, the Spaniards first had to show them that the Spaniards had better weapons.

subjects (SUB-jekts) Subjects are people who live under the rule and protection of a king or queen. Spaniards said the Native Americans they conquered were subjects of the king of Spain.

traverse (truh-VERSS) People traverse something when they walk through it. Coronado and his men traversed many miles of desert, forest, and prairie.

viceroy (VICE-roy) A viceroy rules in place of the king in a faraway land. Antonio de Mendoza ruled Mexico as viceroy for the king of Spain.

Books

Crisfield, Deborah. *Francisco de Coronado.* Austin, Tex.: Raintree Steck-Vaughn
Publishers, 2001.

Nardo, Don. *Francisco Coronado.* New York: Franklin Watts, 2001.

Weisberg, Barbara. *Coronado's Golden Quest.* Austin, Tex.: Steck-Vaughn
Company, 1993.

Whiting, Jim. *Francisco Vásquez de Coronado.* Bear, Del.: Mitchell Lane
Publishers, 2003.

Web Sites

Visit our Web page for lots of links about Francisco Vásquez de Coronado:
http://www.childsworld.com/links.html

***Note to parents, teachers, and librarians: We routinely monitor our Web
links to make sure they're safe, active sites.***

Sources Used by the Author

Bolton, Herbert E. *Coronado: Knight of Pueblos and Plains.* Albuquerque,
N.Mex.: The University of New Mexico Press, 1990.

Cabeza de Vaca, Álvar Núñez. *The Journey of Álvar Núñez Cabeza de Vaca: And
His Companions from Florida to the Pacific 1528–1536.* Translated by
Fanny Bandelier. Edited by Ad. F. Bandelier. New York: A. S. Barnes &
Company, 1905.

de Castañeda, Pedro. *The Journey of Coronado.* Published online.
http://www.pbs.org/weta/thewest/resources/archives/one/corona1.htm

de Coronado, Francisco Vásquez . Letters to Viceroy Mendoza and King of
Spain. Published online.
http://www.pbs.org/weta/thewest/resources/archives/one/corona8.htm

Preston, Douglas. *Cities of Gold.* New York: Simon & Schuster, 1992.

Udall, Stewart L. *To the Inland Empire: Coronado and Our Spanish Legacy.* New
York: Doubleday, 1987.